OLD TOWN NIAGARA: A HISTORY

In July 1999, the Board of The Friends of Fort George directed me, as then President, to liaise with representatives of the other heritage groups in town to consider the concept of applying to have the Town of Niagara designated as a National Historic District.

A Citizens' Heritage Designation Committee was struck. For 15 months the Committee researched the history of Niagara-on-the-Lake and prepared in late 2000, this illustrated submission for designation to the Historic Sites and Monuments Board of Canada.

In May 2004 it was announced that Niagara-on-the-Lake would indeed be designated a National Historic District - the first in Ontario!

The Publications Committee of the Friends of Fort George felt it would be worthwhile to make available to the public this comprehensive, yet very readable, history of this remarkable town.

Richard D. Merritt, Chairman
Publications Committee
The Friends of Fort George

This book is dedicated to the memory of
Frank McDowell Hawley (1916 - 2004),
who was instrumental in the preservation of
the architectural heritage of this town.

Printed and bound in Canada.

Canadian Cataloguing in Publication Data

Editors: The Heritage Designation Committee

ISBN 0-9699298-2-X

The Friends of Fort George National Historic Park Inc.

P.O. Box 1283, Niagara-on-the-Lake, Ontario, L0S 1J0, Canada
ffg@computan.on.ca

Table of Contents

NOVEMBER 2000
EXECUTIVE SUMMARY

Niagara-on-the-Lake (henceforth NOTL) has been known under several other names, the most important of which were Newark and Niagara, but in this submission it will be referred to only by its current name. NOTL is located at the mouth of the Niagara River and the town's boundaries of 1823 are the boundaries of this request for designation.

The proposal is to have the old town declared a national historic district. The reasons for this request as well as documentation are presented fully in the attached historical brief prepared by a committee drawn from all of the town's heritage organizations. The committee believes that the development and characteristics of NOTL are highly significant for provincial, national and even international history. It was one of the first European settlements in what is now Ontario and its story is both a consequence and symbol of the growth of the Canadian nation and of its relations with the United States. A good deal of Ontario and Canada's history can be understood from examining sites within the town as well as its present location and the layout of the town. We believe that few other towns in Canada possess such historical importance with so many facets as does NOTL.

The report is presented under seven themes:
1. Native history; 2. Military history; 3. Refugees and immigrants; 4. Economic development; 5. Political, cultural, and social development; 6. Built heritage; 7. Vox Populi. Here follows a brief discussion of each theme.

Native presence on the site of NOTL extends back in time approximately 10,000 years with the result that the area is rich in artifacts from many different eras. When the French arrived in the early 17th century, an Iroquoian-speaking people lived here and enjoyed a far-flung trading network. The area has seen warfare and dispersal of its native inhabitants until the Anishinabe or Ojibwa (known as Mississauga or Chippewa in southern Ontario) occupied it at the end of the 17th century. The British Crown in order to gain orderly control of the territory along the Niagara River made treaties with both the Iroquoian Senecas and with the Mississaugas. This town and its area have been the location of peaceful and of warlike relations among native peoples as well as between them and Europeans and between them and Americans.

Many of these relations are included under the Military History heading. Here is a site that has had experience of warfare and of other military activity from the time before there was a Canadian nation up to the present. The town is located opposite Fort Niagara. It began the early 18th century as an important French fortified trading post and from the middle of that century, acted as the major French military base in the Great Lakes basin. This fort also served later as an important military post for the British and, then, the Americans. The town has the unique distinction of possessing, within its boundaries, three forts: Fort George dating from 1796, Butlers Barracks dating from 1814 and Fort Mississauga dating from 1814. Along with these are military reserves that provide the town with open spaces for a variety of uses. The town's military past includes serving as a base for invasion of the United States and suffering the experience of foreign occupation and of total destruction by enemy forces. We know of no other town or city in Canada that has passed through such events or that enjoys the presence of three forts with the "enemy" fort within view across the international border.

Even more important in the town's military history is the human dimension. Here there have been native warriors, as well as United Empire Loyalist fighters and French, British, Canadian and American regulars. The original settlement of the town (1778) was a military decision and many of its earliest residents were disbanded citizen-soldiers. The town has seen the training of soldiers for important events in Canada's military (and political) history, e.g., Fenian raids, the Boer War, World War One, World War Two, and modern peacekeeping duties. Among those trained here were hundreds of men for a Polish government-in-exile army and some of those remain in a special burial plot in the cemetery of St. Vincent de Paul Church. For more than two centuries, the civilian residents of the town have suffered and benefitted from warfare and military activity.
The earliest permanent residents of NOTL were refugees and that

aspect of Ontario's (and Canada's) history is well-illustrated in the town's history. Refugees include native peoples, Americans and people of African descent. The town has seen slavery and the fight against it. Town residents have also included people dispossessed or severely distressed in their homelands, such as the Irish or Miss Rye's "waifs and strays." A unique feature of the town has been its ready acceptance of different groups of people finding a new home in Niagara.

Economically, NOTL has a varied, complex history that is reflected in many other southern Ontario centres. The town has been a marketing and distributing centre for local agricultural products; it has been a commercial fishing base; it has possessed a variety of major manufacturing industries. From the late 18th century up to the present, it has seen visitors staying or passing through. NOTL is now a major destination for tourists and much of their interest is in the historic character and associations of the old town. The residents over two centuries have known both great prosperity and deep poverty. While the town now gives the impression of wealth and comfort, traces of less prosperous times can still be found in some locations. The story of boom and bust, of changing economic circumstances and of ways of making a living, all this can be seen in NOTL.

Politically, NOTL has known the heights and lower levels. Within a few years of its founding, it became the first capital of the new province of Upper Canada (thus, Ontario's first capital). The first provincial legislature met here and passed legislation of great and lasting importance. Also associated with this town are some early figures who sought political reform. After it ceased to be the provincial capital, NOTL served as the District capital until 1862, after which it sank into political insignificance.

But, the town made up in other ways for its lack of political importance. It enjoyed a rich cultural and social life from its early days and this continued, with its ebbs and flows, up to the present. It now boasts a major North American theatre season and its residents include many artists and writers, some with international reputations.

For a town of its size its built heritage and its streetscapes may be second to none in Canada. The town's layout demonstrates 18th century town planning and any visitor can discover the pattern because it is obvious visually and the town is small enough to be covered by walking. The buildings date from post-1814, but some in style and location on their lots reflect earlier concepts. Another reflection of earlier periods is the intermingling of residential, commercial and institutional structures. The range of architectural styles is wide and, fortunately, many buildings remain to give a sense of our history. The town and its structures have frequently been the subject of research and writing for both scholarly and popular audiences. The town's built heritage has been recorded by prominent restoration architect, Peter Stokes, a resident who continues to play a major role in restoration in the community and beyond.

Vox Populi deals with the activity of town residents who have created a tradition of citizen activism that may be unsurpassed in Canada. The demand by residents that their views be heard by government and their determination to protect their heritage demonstrate a strength of will that has remained constant over two centuries.

It is clear that the old town of Niagara-on-the-Lake is a district of national historic significance as a microcosm of the history of Ontario. The major themes of the province's history with a couple of exceptions (forestry and mining) are reflected in the story of the old town and graphically illustrated by its extant cultural resources. The old town gives visitors a sense of place, the feeling that they are indeed in an historic town. The broad streets have their modern intrusions as one would expect of a living historic community but the sense is that history walks beside you.

NATIVE HISTORY

The settlement, movement, dispersal and cultural development of native peoples in the Niagara Peninsula reflect very similar changes in the rest of southern Ontario.

The Niagara Peninsula has been home to people for approximately 10,000 years. The first inhabitants were stone-age people, designated by archaeologists as "Paleo-Indians" and they were followed by the "Archaic" people from about 8000 BC to 1000 BC. Artifacts from the Middle Archaic period (c.4000 BC) have been found at Fort George, King's Point, and the Butler homestead site. The next period, the "Woodland," began with the introduction of pottery manufacture and it saw an increasingly complex society and economy. The next cultural period began around AD 500 when corn-growing indicated the beginning of agriculture. That became an increasingly important source of food supplemented by foods that were gathered as well as from hunting and fishing. The period known as the "Princess Point Culture" saw larger and more permanent camps or villages. The "Terminal Woodland" period lasted from about AD 900 to the arrival of Europeans in the 17th century.

The first to arrive were the French when Etienne Brulé reached the land of the Neutral nation in 1615 and Samuel de Champlain probably passed through this area between 1615 and 1618. (HAC, I, pl.36) He used the term la nation neutre to designate the Iroquoian people living here because they remained neutral in the conflicts between the Five Nations Iroquois to the east of their territory and the Iroquoian Hurons to the north. In fact, the Neutrals traded with both peoples as well as with those farther away, e.g., the Wenro-Andastes-Eries to the south and beyond (as far as the Ohio and Mississippi Rivers). The Neutrals like other native peoples, suffered from diseases to which they had no immunity. (HAC, I, pl.35)

After the League of the Iroquois dispersed the Hurons in the years 1647-49, they turned their attention to the Neutrals and in 1651-52 dispersed them as well. (HAC, I, pl.35). The Senecas (one of the Five Nations) gained control of this area, but did not establish permanent settlements. They, in turn, were displaced near the end of the 17th century by Anishinabe or Ojibwa (known as Mississauga or Chippewa in southern Ontario). Perhaps the most enduring legacy of the Neutrals is their name for the river – Onguiaahara – which has been transformed into the word Niagara.

Artifacts from all major Native cultures who have lived in Niagara have been found in Niagara-on-the-Lake.

The transfer of land in Canada from native peoples to the British Crown began in the 1760s when treaties were made between the peoples claiming ownership of territory along the Niagara River and the Crown. The policy was to restrict native land acquisitions to the Crown and not to allow private individuals or groups to be the initial buyers. The Royal Proclamation of 1763 made the policy official and the first purchases were made in 1764 when the Senecas granted to the British government a strip two miles wide on the west side of the river from Lake Ontario to the top of the Niagara Escarpment. In 1781 by treaty with the Mississaugas, this strip was widened to four miles and extended from Lake Ontario to Lake Erie. (OHM, Map 4.2) This policy of Crown acquisition was to be followed throughout Ontario in later years and was extended to western Canada.

References

Historical Atlas of Canada, I, plates 6, 7, 8, 9, 12, 14, 18, 38, 39
Ontario History in Maps
A. Rotstein, "The Mystery of the Neutral Indians," in Patterns of the Past. Interpreting Ontario's History. Edited by R.Hall, W.Westfall and L.S.MacDowell (Toronto & Oxford: Dundurn Press, 1988)

Niagara on the Lake
Canada
The Niagara-on-the-Lake "Times" Christmas Souvenir.
PICKWELL BROS., Publishers.

MILITARY HISTORY

Niagara has seen military history from at least 1726 when the French built a stone building on the east bank of the Niagara River at the point where it flows into Lake Ontario. The French had obtained Seneca approval for a trading post, but this building was much stronger than what was needed simply for trade and so it established a French military presence in the area. The garrison of this fort crossed to the west bank, where the old town now stands, and established cultivated fields of crops. [1760 map] The French expanded Fort Niagara and it played an important role in the wars between the British and French for control of Canada until the British finally captured it in 1759. The fort continued to expand in area and complexity as later owners – the British and Americans – found it strategically important in several wars. Fort Niagara can be viewed from the old town of NOTL and is a constant reminder of a long history both warlike and peaceful. The relationship with the United States whether stormy or friendly has obviously had tremendous impact on Ontario and Canada.

During the American War for Independence, Fort Niagara became an important base for operations against the rebellious colonies. From here British regulars accompanied by loyal American soldiers of Butler's Rangers and war parties of Seneca and Cayuga men raided the frontier settlements of the colonies. Large numbers of men, women and children, including native peoples made homeless by the conflict, gathered at Niagara, starving and with little more than the clothes on their backs. These refugees strained the food stores of the fort. Consequently, in 1778, the British commander sent John Butler to begin farming on the west side of the Niagara River. The log buildings that his Rangers constructed formed the first structures of the later old town and the few Loyalist families who began to grow crops were the first civilian settlers on the west bank. When the American Revolution ended in 1783, the military no longer needed the settlement to feed Fort Niagara, but a permanent European-type settlement had been established and would persist. When Butler's Rangers were disbanded in 1784, many settled with their families in and near the boundaries of the later old town and they formed "the first permanent British settlement in western Quebec." (HAC, II, Plate 7)

The wave of Loyalist settlers, perhaps 50,000 in total to British North America, caused major changes in government, economy and society and NOTL was one starting point for those changes. The town remained a military centre where officers of the garrison shared with the populace their interests in music, dances, concerts, and plays. Together, the military and civilian inhabitants established a pattern for a town still known for its culture and elegance.

When Fort Niagara was turned over to the Americans in1796, the British government authorized the construction of Fort George. This fort firmly established British military presence on the west side of the Niagara River and that presence, supported by this fortification, would be a major reason for American attacks on the area and for successful defence of Upper Canada. That, in turn, was a major reason why Canada remained independent of the United States. Fort George was the headquarters of the British army in southern Ontario and the main depot of the British Indian Department whose officials held large councils with the native population on the Commons surrounding the fort. (OHM, Map 2.6 shows the strategic importance of the town site.)

At the outbreak of the War of 1812, Major-General Isaac Brock made his headquarters at Fort George and he returned there after his victory at Detroit to prepare for an expected American invasion. When the Americans invaded across the Niagara River against Queenston (13 October), he hurried from Fort George, but was killed leading his troops in battle on Queenston Heights. Six Nations warriors under John Norton left from the area of the fort and after reaching the Heights, began to skirmish with the Americans. The warriors not only prevented the invaders from advancing but also frightened large numbers of militiamen on the other side of the river. Brock's successor, Major-General Roger Sheaffe, meanwhile gathered his forces and led them to Queenston where, on the Heights, he defeated the Americans late in the afternoon. The Americans in Fort Niagara turned their guns on Fort George and on the town, setting several buildings on fire including the roof of the stone powder magazine at the fort. The town and fort were in great danger because the magazine held enough powder, if it exploded, to destroy both. Racing against time, a few volunteers quelled the flames before they could reach the powder. Many examples of bravery that made a difference to Ontario's future can be cited and this was certainly one of them. That very powder magazine, the oldest military building in Ontario, can still be visited. Following the Battle of Queenston Heights, a short truce was negotiated and Brock and his aide-de-camp, Lieutenant-Colonel John Macdonell, were buried in a state funeral in one of the bastions of Fort George.

On 25 May, 1813, the American fleet in the mouth of the Niagara River supported by the guns of Fort Niagara opened up a massive bombardment of Fort George. Red hot cannonballs and exploding shells soon set the fort's wooden buildings on fire. Within a few hours every building in the fort and at Navy Hall was consumed – except for the stone powder magazine. Two days later, several thousand American soldiers, protected by the guns of their fleet, landed on the Lake Ontario shore, west of the fort. The battle advanced from the lakeshore through the town until finally the British force of regulars, militia and native warriors was driven out. The American occupation of the fort and town had begun. They built defensive earthworks in the town (some remains can still be seen in St. Mark's Church cemetery) and strengthened Fort George. The Americans tried to advance westward along the lakeshore but were turned back at Stoney Creek and tried to advance inland, but were defeated at Beaver Dams. Throughout the summer and autumn, the Americans were kept locked up at Niagara, unable to exploit their bridgehead to capture any more territory. Native warriors, militiamen and British regulars continually attacked their sentries and ambushed their patrols.

The Americans reduced the garrison at Niagara and on 10 December, their commander gave orders to withdraw across the river to Fort Niagara. First, however, he ordered the town burned and the inhabitants were given only a few hours notice before they were forced out into the snow to watch their homes torched. Niagara experienced the horror of warfare against unarmed civilians that few other parts of Canada have known.

The British took revenge by capturing Fort Niagara and then by burning the American communities all along the river, including Buffalo.

In 1814, the American army invaded and after defeating the British at Chippawa advanced toward the town of Niagara. They threatened it while waiting for the fleet to arrive. It did not and the invaders withdrew to Chippawa. Soon after, the British and American forces met at Lundy's Lane and fought the fiercest land battle of the war. The town did not witness any more fighting, but it had suffered greatly from the war. Many men had been wounded, killed or imprisoned, homes and buildings had been reduced to ashes, fruit trees had been cut down, and livestock driven off.

The British army quickly began to rebuild Fort George while adding two new military installations, Fort Mississauga and Butler's Barracks. Because Fort George did not command the entrance to the mouth of the Niagara River, Mississauga was intended to correct that fault. A star-shaped fortification, the fort was dominated by a massive brick tower, part of which was built from stone and brick salvaged from the destroyed town of Niagara. Butler's Barracks was built on the other side of the Fort George common, out of cannon range of the American shore, for it was to become the main depot of the military establishment. The old town may be unique in Canada in having three forts within its boundaries and a clear view of a nearby American fort. All of these military structures convey a great deal of the meaning of the history of the area and of relations between Canada and the United States. Their spatial relationships to each other extend beyond their military significance into such areas as diplomacy, politics and economics. For example, while they owe their creation to war or fear of war, they now symbolize peaceful relations between the neighbouring countries and attract great numbers of visitors from both sides of the border as well as from abroad.

When rebellion, led by William Lyon Mackenzie, broke out in Toronto in 1837, many Niagara men who were opposed to it formed themselves into militia companies. A group of Niagara firemen commandeered a steamer and sailed to the capital to aid in its defence. Fort Mississauga was reinforced. Local militiamen including a company of black residents stood guard over the frontier and the Welland Canal but no attacks came. During the 1840s, 1850s and 1860s several companies of the Royal Canadian Rifles were posted to Niagara, thus making it the Regiment's headquarters.

Number One Company, Niagara Volunteers was formed early in 1861 under the authority of the Militia Act of 1854.

The next time that there appeared to be a threat of attack came with the Civil War in the United States. Fort Niagara was strengthened and reinforced and "crimps" (men and women trying to gain a bounty by recruiting young Canadian men for the Union army) were active all along the Canadian side of the river. Britain and the United States came dangerously close to war as a result of the raid on St. Albans, Vermont and the activities of Confederate agents in Canada. The British responded by garrisoning Fort Mississauga and putting the troops at Butler's Barracks on alert. As well, the Niagara Volunteers were put on guard along the Niagara River and, near the end of the Civil War, were sent to help protect the border at Phillipsburg, Quebec.

After the end of the Civil War, the American Fenian Brotherhood sought to instigate war between Britain and the United States. To this end, it threatened Canada and even launched invasions at several points including against Fort Erie. Again, Niagara militia companies were called up and they reinforced the troops at Fort Mississauga and Butler's Barracks. The Niagara Volunteers went to Fort Erie as part of the 19th Battalion from St. Catharines, but were not involved in fighting. When the Fenians again threatened to invade in 1870, Number One Company spent some time guarding the Welland Canal. HAC, II, Plate 24, shows British garrisons to 1871 with Niagara shown as a major garrison. This would rank it with Quebec and Halifax and equaled in Ontario only by Kingston.

After the Fenian threat ended, Britain and the U.S. sought to establish more permanent peaceful relations (e.g., the 1871 Treaty of Washington); consequently, British garrisons were withdrawn from Canada. The forts of Niagara and the military lands were turned over to Canada, forcing the new country to provide for its own defence. In 1871, Butler's Barracks and the Commons at Niagara became Camp Niagara, a massive summer militia training camp. It had a major impact on the town because thousands of troops lived in tents on the Commons during the summer. At Camp Niagara thousands of young men were trained for service in both World Wars.

In World War I, one group was unique. A Polish government in exile was formed and it undertook to form a Polish army recruited from men of Polish descent in the United States. The costs were to be paid by France and the training was to take place in Canada. Beginning in 1917, hundreds of young Polish Americans and Canadians arrived in Niagara and were billeted in buildings in the town. A number of these men died here, including twenty-six who succumbed to the great influenza epidemic in 1919, and were buried in a special memorial plot in the St. Vincent de Paul Church cemetery. The burial site remains dedicated to these young men and each year in June, Polish Sunday involves a memorial service to remember them.

In 1922, the Clock Tower was erected on Queen Street as a war memorial to the Niagara men who died during the Great War. During the 1930s, as a make-work project, reconstruction of Fort George was undertaken. It was completed by 1940 but war delayed its opening for visitors for five years.

Throughout the Second World War, Camp Niagara was a hub of activity with troops stationed here to protect the hydro facilities of Niagara Falls and the vital transportation link of the Welland Canal. Thousands of men of the Canadian Army and women of the Canadian Women's Army Corps called the town home during the war years. In addition, the local airport was part of the Commonwealth Air Training Plan.

When the war ended, more names were added to the Town War Memorial Clock Tower. Fort George was officially opened in 1950 and Camp Niagara continued in use for the next two decades with all local militia units using the Commons for training at summer camp. The last official use was in 1965, but the militia presence continues with the recently opened Lincoln and Welland Regiment Museum in one of the buildings of Butler's Barracks.

The military presence has been continuous since 1778 when Butler's Rangers first moved into their barracks on the west shore of the Niagara River. Canadians trained in this town fought in the War of 1812, Upper Canadian Rebellion, Fenian Raids, Northwest Rebellion, Boer War, World War I, World War II, Korea and other actions. A few of the peacekeepers of modern times had their first taste of military life at Camp Niagara.

The military sites remain preserved by Parks Canada: Fort Mississauga, Fort George, Navy Hall, Butler's Barracks, Brock's Monument. All are within or very close to the old town and are evocative treasures recalling the struggles and sacrifices to keep Canada free.

References

"The Military in Niagara" Advance Historical Issue, Spring 1980
Niagara Historical Society, pamphlet no.35, J.Carnochan, "The Polish Army in Niagara"
Niagara-on-the-Lake Canada. (John S.Clarke publisher, [1904])

CELEBRATION OF EMANCIPATION ACT

Niagara-on-the-Lake
Ontario, Canada

1793–1993

A PLACE OF REFUGE

3.1 The Loyalists

In the 1770s the first significant numbers of refugees appeared in Canada and one of their major locations was along the Niagara River. They were native peoples and American Loyalists including black people. Thus, this town from the time of its first settlement by Europeans to the present has been a refuge for many people for a variety of reasons.

Major John Butler built barracks here in the winter of 1778 and a hospital and additional log houses in the spring of 1779. In the summer of that year, he began a pilot food production project, settling three or four refugee families to clear land.

Shortage of food was a problem in 1778 and it became critical in the fall of 1779 as American General Sullivan invaded Six Nations territory, burning towns and crops, and driving thousands of aboriginal people to the fort to seek refuge. By October, almost 4,000 native peoples were drawing rations at Fort Niagara. (Wilson, 79)

In order to alleviate the food shortage, more and more refugees joined the farming community on the west bank. In August 1782 sixteen families, comprising 85 persons, had cleared 236 acres for crops.

After the war, the west bank became a refuge for hundreds of disbanded Rangers, Indian Department officers and men, and for some of their Six Nations allies. In May 1784, forty-six families had cleared more than 700 acres and Colonel De Peyster's list of settlers and those wishing to settle, dated July 1784, notes a total of 620 persons. Several other lists of settlers and prospective settlers exist. They show that the Loyalists were a multicultural group. Six Nations refugees settled along the Grand River (1784-85) and elsewhere in Upper Canada.

3.2 People of African Descent

Niagara is one of the few towns in Ontario to have had people of African descent in its population from the beginning of the province. The 1782 census of Niagara includes one male slave and the 1783 census seven males and three females. There were also by the 1790s, black males who had earned freedom fighting with the loyalists.

The anti-slavery legislation of 1793 paved the way for an influx of blacks from the United States before the Underground Railroad became active. This legislation was triggered by events involving two of Niagara's Black residents – Chloe Cooley and Peter Martin. Chloe's master had brutally bound her and despite her resistance, taken her across the Niagara River in order to sell her. In March 1793, her case was brought before Simcoe's Executive Council and one of the two witnesses who testified was Peter Martin, a free man. Simcoe and Council members Chief Justice William Osgoode and Receiver General Peter Russell could take no legal action because slavery was not illegal. Simcoe, however, was encouraged to work against slavery and he had Chief Justice Osgoode draft the anti-slavery legislation that was passed in June of that year. In many ways the African American experience in Niagara-on-the-Lake mirrored that in other small Ontario towns, but Niagara alone can claim to have provided a major impetus for the ending of slavery in Canada.

Two Niagarans of African descent, James and Humphrey Waters, received Crown grants to lots in the old town in 1795, becoming the founding fathers of the town's "coloured village." In 1830, the town had an estimated twenty-two black residents and by 1842, eighty-two. Stories of their difficult journeys to Niagara and their joy on arriving are part of the town's history.

In 1837, the town witnessed the Solomon Moseby (Molesby, Mosely) affair. He escaped on horseback from slavery in Kentucky and left the horse before reaching Canada. His former slave-master obtained an arrest warrant on grounds of horse theft and Solomon was placed in the Niagara jail to await extradition to the United States. After three weeks and in spite of two petitions against extradition, the Lieutenant Governor ordered the local sheriff to arrange to return Moseby to Kentucky. Led by a local schoolteacher and preacher, Hubert

Holmes, several hundred "people of colour" gathered to prevent Moseby's removal. The sheriff placed Moseby in a wagon but Holmes and another man, Jacob Green, stopped it. Both were seriously wounded by soldiers in the scuffle and later died and were buried in the "Negro Burial Ground" at the south edge of town where the former Baptist Church stood. During the noisy demonstration, Moseby escaped, never to be recaptured. This protest against extradition of a refugee slave, helped to establish the legal principle in Canada that refugee slaves would not be extradited to the United States solely on grounds that they had fled from slavery. This principle meant that slaves would find legal freedom in Canada and that condition was the foundation for the Underground Railroad.

The Underground Railroad brought more freedom seekers. In 1851, the town had 94 black residents and 104 in 1861. Most of them owned a house and lot, had regular jobs and very few became indigents or law breakers. Some were very successful, particularly two sons of Humphrey Waters. One owned a successful livery while the other accumulated twenty-three acres of land in town and won several elections to Town Council. Both owned substantial houses, at least three of which survive.

Mary Ann Shadd, editor of the Provincial Freeman, noted in 1854 that the town's "coloured citizens are prosperous. Nearly every family possessing a homestead. There is no prejudice." This lack of prejudice had been evident almost from the beginning on both sides. Some of the town's black residents served in the Coloured Corps in 1812-14 and others served in 1838 and later with the Incorporated Militia protecting the Welland Canal. White residents were equally ready to help black citizens. In 1837, 117 whites signed a petition protesting the decision to send Solomon Moseby back to Kentucky, and some individuals, particularly Peter Servos, helped families to escape the United Stages and to get settled in Niagara. Intermarriage was not frowned upon. For example, Humphrey Waters married Catherine Servos (aunt of Peter) and three of his sons married white women.

In 1999, the Niagara Foundation purchased a house built c.1835 by one of Niagara's black residents. The Foundation intends to restore it. Several other houses once occupied by black citizens also survive.

Niagara was one destination for slaves fleeing to freedom both before and after the Underground Railroad started and what happened here can, in many ways, be taken as representative of what was occurring elsewhere in Upper Canada.

3.3 Political and Economic Refugees

Several French royalist emigrés came from England to Newark/NOTL. In 1792, Pierre (Peter) Desjardins arrived and worked for a local merchant. He moved to other places and worked for other employers, but continued to own property in the town at the corner of Queen and Simcoe streets until his death in 1827. Desjardins is remembered as being the promoter of a canal to connect the town of Dundas with Burlington Bay. He borrowed money to have the canal dug, petitioned for ownership of the land and received it. Although work on the Desjardin Canal continued until 1837, it could not match the Burlington Bay Canal which opened in 1826 and gave Dundas' rival, Hamilton, easy access to Lake Ontario.

In 1797, the Comte de Puisaye, an aristocrat who had fled to England, applied to the government for permission to form a settlement of fellow aristocrats in Upper Canada. He and his associates presented a scheme that promised repayment of public expenses and the creation of self-supporting colonists in Canada who would help to defend British rule there. As the vanguard of an expected migration of thousands of French royalists, the count brought forty-one French Royalists in 1798 and they were granted land north of York. He left his emigrés in 1799 and bought "Mr. Sheehan's place on the Niagara river." Part of the house he built there survives.

The Irish were part of the British migration to Canada that began in 1815, after the Napoleonic Wars. While mainly Ulster Protestants, there were many Catholics amongst them. The animosity between these two groups elsewhere in the province does not appear to have afflicted this town. Adherents to both sides assisted with the erection of St. Andrew's Presbyterian, St. Mark's Anglican and St. Vincent de Paul Catholic churches.

Some of these early immigrants were veterans of the Irish regiments that were reduced after the end of hostilities. Later Irish were mainly labourers, although some engaged in trade. They maintained their homogeneity by settling in the area of town bounded by Paffard, Rye, Niagara and Charlotte streets, which became known as Irishtown.

The peak immigration occurred during the 1830s and 1840s, leading up to the great influx in 1847-49 caused by the potato famine. As Niagara was a busy port on Lake Ontario, it was natural that many immigrants arrived at our docks, seeking work at the Niagara Harbour and Dock company, and remained in town. Many of these arrivals carried disease and in 1847 forty died at Niagara. The Police Board (the body that administered the town) received orders to form a Board of Health. Medical officers were appointed and buildings were rented for a hospital and for shelter. An inspector visited the steamboats on arrival to examine the passengers. The Niagara Chronicle of 16 July, 1847, records that there were still several cases of fever in the hospital. Poor sanitary conditions on the immigrant ships had brought about an outbreak of cholera which eventually spread throughout Canada East (Quebec) and Canada West (Ontario). Thousands died.

At the end of the American Civil War, a few Confederates sought temporary refuge in Niagara. The best known of these was Senator Mason, one of the principals in the Trent affair. In 1867, Jefferson Davis visited and was greeted warmly by the town council and town band. Other Confederates were General Breckenridge who lived on Front Street, as did General Hood and Colonel Love. General Early boarded at Mr. Barker's on Johnson Street. Colonel Taylor and General Palfrey were other important ex-Confederate military men who found their way to the town. Other Southerners who came were James Clay (son of Henry), C. Hellems (former American Consul at Havana) and Mr. Porterfield of Nashville. Three ministers who arrived were Rev. Mr. Inslee, the Presbyterian Rev. Stuart Robinson and the Episcopalian Rev. Dr. Leacock (of New Orleans) who preached at St. Mark's during his sojourn in town.

At least three of their domiciles remain: the former Doritty house on King St., leased by Rev. Leacock and his daughter Mrs. Grey, the widow of a Confederate officer; Senator Mason's rented house on Wellington St. near St. Mark's; and, the Barker house at Regent and Johnson Streets which General Early rented.

Organized juvenile immigration to Ontario had its beginning in Niagara-on-the-Lake in October 1869 when Miss Maria Rye arrived with seventy-five girls from England. Her work was part of a larger canvas, for one great concern of 19th century upper and middle class social reformers in Canada and Britain was the plight of homeless and pauper children. One solution they undertook was to send them in groups to Canada and other dominions. Thus, what happened in Niagara was a sample of what occurred elsewhere in Canada. The movement of organized juvenile immigration aroused controversy over motives, methods and consequences for the children and Maria Rye was at the centre of much of the debate.

The previous year, she had bought the town's second jail and courthouse and converted it into "Our Western Home" (OWH). Here she brought the first group of girls aged four to twelve. (She intended to restrict her work to girls, but brought the occasional boy.) Her example was soon followed by many others and the movement in Ontario and other provinces lasted until it was ended by the Great Depression in the 1930s. The majority of children sent by Maria Rye were taken from workhouses where she assumed they would have received some schooling or training; others were homeless children taken from the streets. The intention of Maria Rye and her supporters was to have the children adopted by Canadian families or apprenticed until age eighteen. OWH was to be a temporary shelter providing some training in domestic work and a distribution centre.

Maria Rye had high level supporters such as the Archbishop of Canterbury and Sir John A. Macdonald. To provide local supervision of the children and the families that took them, she relied on prominent citizens such as Henry Paffard, the mayor of Niagara, Robert Ball, a Justice of the Peace and Rev. Dr. McMurray, the vicar of St. Mark's church. Other local supporters included William Kirby, editor of the Niagara Mail, the Alma family, John W. Ball, Edward and James Hiscott, Dr. Anderson, Dr. Morson and Senator Josiah B. Plumb.

By 1874, Rye had brought over 800 children and as the numbers increased rapidly, questions were being asked about follow-up supervision. Andrew Doyle investigated on behalf of the British government and criticized Rye's operation for failing to look out for the children's interests. Consequently, for two years, she ceased to bring children and then resumed the work until retiring in 1896 by which time "she claimed to have resettled over 4000 English pauper girls in Canada." (Diamond, xvii) Her work was taken over by the Church of England's Waifs and Strays Society and it continued to use OWH until just after World War 1.

In the 1890s, partly out of concern for immigrant children, Ontario passed legislation to protect children and established the Children's Aid Society with J.J.Kelso as its first president. He wrote a report (1897) on the immigration of British children and was critical of Rye's efforts: "the work has not been properly handled in the past and… some radical change would be necessary before it could be considered satisfactory from a Canadian standpoint. The arrangements…for the supervision of the children after going to foster homes and situations were far from adequate. Miss Rye, …did not make any effort to have the children personally visited after leaving her care, and she is credited with the statement that the other homes were going to an unnecessary expense in maintaining a staff of visitors. …… These four thousand children have gone to all parts of Ontario, but probably a large proportion find homes in the Niagara district." (Wagner, 156)

Our Western Home had an impact on the town because Rye bought supplies and food from local stores and hired local people for both inside and outside tasks. The children attended St. Mark's Church, but in the years 1902 to 1912, the Home's policy was to avoid contact between the girls and town residents. Although the Home was demolished several years ago, some evidence of Miss Rye's presence remains. At the south end of King St., opposite the site of OWH, a brick house purchased by Miss Rye in 1872 to house girls who had been returned to the home, has been carefully restored as a private residence. (The object of housing them there was to prevent their influencing other girls adversely.) In the cemetery of St. Mark's there is an OWH plot, marked by a Celtic cross, and it is the resting place of five girls and one boy brought to Canada by Miss Rye and of Miss Bayley, her successor.

The experiences of immigrant children, whether brought by Maria Rye or by others, covered the range from happy to unhappy, from success to failure, but those who remained in Canada contributed to the development of the country.

Americans sought refuge from summer heat and pollution in their cities in the late 19th and early 20th centuries. These summer residents built new houses and enlarged and renovated older ones, usually festooning them with large verandahs where they could enjoy the lake breezes. A promotional booklet published by the town in 1904 to advertise its fresh air, modern sanitation, and "absence of rowdies" features photos of many of the summer estates. There are obvious comparisons with the resort era in Cobourg and perhaps with towns along the St. Lawrence.

Many of the grand houses remain, including three significant groups: the buildings on north west Queen St. facing the golf course and the lake; three houses at the Queen/Simcoe St. intersection; and, three houses on John St. east. They comprise the nucleus of Niagara's estate lots.

Some 20,000 Mennonites came to Canada in the 1920s and a small number settled in Vineland. One of that group, Peter Wall (for whom a local road is named) bought 400 acres in Niagara township, dividing it into smaller lots which were bought by other Mennonites. After World War II, Mennonites came from Paraguay, Brazil, and Argentina. They generally settled in the township, but had impacts on the town - economically, socially and politically. They helped found the Niagara Fruit Co-operative and the Niagara Credit Union; the town has elected two Mennonite Lord Mayors, two Members of Parliament and one Member of Provincial Parliament as well as aldermen. The Mennonites have four churches and one of their former churches was moved to town in the 1960s for use as a Boy Scout Hall.

References

D.H.Akenson, The Irish in Ontario. A Study in Rural History (Kingston & Montreal: McGill-Queen's University Press, 1984)

Bicentennial Stories of Niagara-on-the-Lake. Edited by John L. Field (Lincoln, Ont: 1981)

H. R. Bergman "The Niagara Area Mennonites"

Canada Land of Immigrants, Nelson Canadian Studies Series: P Watson ed.

The Capital Years. Niagara-on-the-Lake, 1792-1796. Edited by Richard Merritt, Nancy Butler, and Michael Power. (Toronto; Dundurn Press, 1991)

J. Carnochan, History of Niagara (Facsimile edition, 1973)

Marian Diamond, Emigration and Empire: The Life of Maria S.Rye, (New York & London: Garland, 1999)

Dictionary of Canadian Biography, 6 (Desjardins; Puisaye); 7 (see Nelson Hackett biography)

The Doyle Report and Miss Rye's Reply 1875

Daniel G. Hill, The Freedom-Seekers. Blacks in Early Canada (1981)

The Haldimand Papers

Hutchinson & Power, Goaded to Madness, Slabtown Press, St. Catharines 1999

Wm. Kirby Annals of Niagara,

Kirby Papers, Miss Rye's correspondence with Wm.Kirby, Land Board records Lincoln County registry abstracts and memorials

Newspaper columns on Miss Rye from: Niagara Mail (21 April to 8 Dec 1869), Echo of Niagara 1884, Buffalo Express Oct. 1894, Niagara Times (Dec 4 1903)

Newspaper columns on Confederate visitors: The Niagara Mail, June 5, 1867 and The Globe, May 29 & May 31, 1867.

Niagara on the Lake Estate Lots Plan: Nicholas Hill c. 1986

Niagara Historical Society, "Notes on Niagara" #27 and #32, pp.59-60 (on the Irish)

Niagara Historical Society # 21 (French emigres); #4 and #37 (Aboriginal refugees and Loyalists)

Niagara Historical Society Collection

Owen A. Thomas, Niagara's Freedom Trail (1995)

G.C.Patterson, "Land Settlement in Upper Canada, 1783-1840" 16th Report of the Department of Archives of Ontario (1920)

A.J.Rennie, Centennial History, 1967

Miss Rye's reply to Charges of Allendale Grainger 1874

Slavery and Freedom In Niagara, Niagara Historical Society 1993
W. B. Turner, "Organized Juvenile Immigration to Canada: Personal Experiences from the Niagara Peninsula," pp.47-64 in Immigration and Settlement. Proceedings of the Third Annual Niagara Peninsula History Conference. (1981)
Wesley Turner, "Miss Rye's Children and the Ontario Press, Ontario History 68 (Sept. 1976), 169-203
Gillian Wagner, Children of the Empire. (1982)
Bruce Wilson, As She Began. An Illustrated Introduction to Loyalist Ontario (1981)

Niagara Central Ry. Cars leaving Simcoe Park
Niagara-on-the-Lake, Canada

SLAVERY
and
FREEDOM
in NIAGARA

UNION JACK
BRAND
ONE GRADE ONLY
AND
THAT THE BEST
EMPTY CAN AS
SOON AS
OPENED
TRADE MARK
REGISTERED
STRAWBERRIES
PUT UP BY
THE UNION JACK CANNING CO.
NIAGARA-ON-THE-LAKE, ONTARIO, CANADA

UNION JACK
BRAND
ONE GRADE ONLY
AND
THAT THE BEST
EMPTY CAN AS
SOON AS
OPENED
HEAVY SYRUP
STRAWBERRIES

ECONOMIC DEVELOPMENT

4.1 Agriculture

Niagara-on-the-Lake is blessed by a mild micro-climate as a result of the moderating effects of Lake Ontario to the north and the protection of the Niagara escarpment to the south. The longer growing season allows the cultivation of tender fruits such as peaches, apricots and cherries and the development of vinifera grapes for the wine industry.

As with many communities founded in southern Ontario, farming was initially the principal means of making a living. Farmers were concerned about markets, prices, transportation, and facilities (e.g., mills) to process their products. Farmers experienced good times and bad times and had to adapt to meet changing tastes, demands and conditions. What happened in and near NOTL can be taken as a sample of developments elsewhere in Ontario (and, indeed, other parts of Canada). In a recent study, Paul Chapman writes, "Many of the trends apparent in Niagara, such as a decline in the number of farms, changing crop patterns and diminished acreages, mirror similar changes in the agricultural sector which have occurred both province- and nation-wide." (NCL, 283) He points out that although the peninsula is highly urbanized, "Today agriculture is the largest land user in the Region, covering 52% of the land area." (NCL, 279)

The story of agriculture in and near the town, began before 1759, when, on the fertile west bank of the Niagara River, a King's Garden was established by the French.

In 1778, Governor General Haldimand authorized cultivation under Colonel John Butler of the King's Field, a 25-acre plot of cleared land. The government provided rations for two years, farm implements and other necessities for Loyalist settlers. It also recognized the importance of mills, grist to grind grain and saw to cut wood for homes and barns. The government employed Sergeant David Brass to erect the first grist mill (and saw mill) in 1783 on Four Mile Creek and Captain Daniel Servos was put in charge of running it. In the first census, 1782, Butler reported that 238 acres had been cleared and the residents had 45 horses, 55 cattle, 88 hogs, 30 sheep,

206 bushels of wheat, 930 bushels of corn, 46 bushels of oats and 100 bushels of potatoes. The census of the following year showed an increase in the acreage cleared and in the number of farm animals.

These early censuses show that grain and livestock farming predominated yet fruit was grown in the area from its earliest days, for in the 1790s there are references to cherry, peach and apple trees and farmers were importing fruit trees. (Carnochan) Cattermole wrote about the area in the early 1830s, "the climate is favourable to fruit, the finest peaches in the Upper Province are grown there, and sent by steamers daily to York [Toronto], and large quantities of cider and white fish." But fruit and grape farming did not gain wider importance until the 1870s. Apples were the most important crop in the 1880s, but were replaced by peaches by the early 1900s and in the same period, grapes became an increasingly common crop. Although the Niagara Peninsula is now noted for its fruit and grape production, its agriculture has been characterized by diversity.

Within a few years of settlement, pioneer farmers who had started by growing food for local consumption were producing surpluses. They soon produced crops for markets as distant as Montreal. To clear their land, farmers burned many trees and sold the wood ash or potash, much of which was exported down the St. Lawrence River. Farmers needed cash to buy such necessities as salt, tea, metal goods, weapons and gunpowder. As cities expanded and steamboats and trains increased the speed of travel, fresh fruit exports became possible. By the 1870s, apples from this area were being sold on the streets of Glasgow and London.

In 1792 the first agricultural society in Upper Canada began to meet in Niagara and Lieutenant Governor Simcoe served as its patron. The Society bought books on farming (often called "husbandry"). Within a few years, the Society organized fairs to show cattle and provide social activities such as races and banquets. In 1846, the province sponsored the first provincial fair and in 1850, it was held in the town. This fair was discontinued in 1889 and there are gaps in the history of agricultural societies, but essentially, these societies and fairs were the predecessors of today's agricultural fairs held all over Ontario as well as the annual Royal Agricultural Winter Fair held in Toronto.

In 1896 the Delhi Canning Company opened at the old Niagara Harbour and Dock Company. This company was taken over by Dominion Canners. A fruit basket factory was also built in the dock area which became a major port for farmers shipping their fruit by steamer to the Toronto markets.

Greaves Jams is a locally owned business that makes jams, marmalades and relishes using local fruit as much as possible. William Greaves started the business in 1928 in the building still occupied by the company on Queen Street. The products were made there and stored in a warehouse across the street. In 1934, despite the Great Depression, the business was so successful that the Greaves replaced their gas kettle with two large steam kettles. The company still operates the store on Queen Street. Greaves' products are highly regarded and customers come from all over North America to purchase Greaves' products.

In 1975 Inniskillin was granted the first licence since 1929 to produce wine, signaling the beginning of the great expansion of local wineries and the effort to produce fine quality wines. Currently, twelve wineries are located in and near the old town and they are winning a good many national and international awards for their wine. This agricultural industry is an outstanding example of adaption to changing conditions of trade and of consumption.

References:

Agriculture and Farm Life in the Niagara Peninsula. Proceedings of the Fifth Annual Niagara Peninsula History Conference (1983)
Janet Carnochan, History of Niagara (Facsimile edition, 1973)
William Cattermole, Emigration. The Advantages of Emigration to Canada (1831)
Niagara's Changing Landscapes. Edited by H.J.Gayler (1994), NCL

4.2 Fishing

Given the town's location at the Niagara River's outflow into Lake Ontario, it is not surprising that fish would provide a source of food. There is evidence that native peoples set up fishing camps on the west side of the river. References to fish types and fishing increase in number in the second half of the 18th century. Fishing became a major food source. Captain Patrick Campbell in 1792 saw up to 6,000 whitefish a day being caught in seine nets and mentions that inhabitants and troops were regulated as to the days when they could fish. The Duc de La Rochefoucauld-Liancourt in 1795 helped soldiers to net 500 fish, "sturgeons, pike, sunfish, salmon, trout, herring." (NHS, no.11)

Many old town families made a livelihood from commercial fishing which took place from the mouth of the Niagara River to Four Mile Creek along the Lake Ontario shore. Prominent among them was the Ball family. Joseph Masters wrote that "practically all the commercial fishing equipment" was concentrated "between Rousseau's wharf [at the foot of Melville Street] and King Street." Many types of boats were used and several different kinds of nets.

Today, commercial licences are still maintained in town while sports fishing attracts numerous anglers to the mouth of the Niagara River to fish for salmon, lake trout and other species of fish.

References:

Niagara Historical Society pamphlet no.11, "Reminiscences of Niagara"
"Niagara Reminiscences" by Joseph E. Masters on http://historyniagara.niagara.com

4.3 Commerce, Transportation and Shipping

Like many other Upper Canadian lakeshore settlements, shipbuilding activity began early. The first vessels built at Niagara were the sloop *Charity* (1770) and *Caldwell* (1774); gunboats were built in 1779 and 1780. Many vessels followed including the *Lord Nelson* (1811) which was seized by the Americans, renamed *Scourge* and sank in Lake Ontario in August 1813.

The owners of the *Lord Nelson* were James and William Crooks who had formed a partnership in 1797 in Niagara. They engaged in a variety of businesses, "particularly military provisioning, the shipment of grain and flour to Lower Canada, brewing and distilling, and the production of potash." (DCB, 8,185) They chartered vessels and built the *Lord Nelson* to facilitate their business. The W. and J. Crooks partnership is a good example of enterprising merchants whose operations had both local and long distance impacts. Sometimes these businesses soon failed or changed and sometimes they went on to greater growth. James became postmaster at Niagara and married into a prominent local family. His homestead, "Crookstown," was destroyed in 1813. The loss of this and other properties and goods in Niagara brought about the demise of the W. and J. Crooks partnership. James Crooks did well in real estate deals in Niagara and went on to an even more prominent business and political career elsewhere in Upper Canada.

After the War of 1812, except for shipping related businesses, commercial enterprises shifted to Queen Street and Prideaux Street. Niagara was an important forwarding point to ship goods to Lake Erie and beyond until the building of the second Welland Canal allowed ships to travel between Lakes Ontario and Erie. Its location and role as the centre of a district helped promote commerce. The town had many inns, taverns and hotels.

The first resident shipbuilder was Amos Roberts who lived in town from 1823 to 1828. In 1831, a group of local entrepreneurs formed the Niagara Harbour and Dock Company. It was given a crown grant of the waterfront between King and Collingwood Streets and inland to Ricardo Street. They proceeded to dredge and excavate a marshy area at the mouth of the river and to construct a steam railway to haul ships out of the water for repair. In 1833, the Company launched its first ship, the *Princess Victoria*, from this yard. They also operated a ship repair business, hauling the *Canada* ashore for repairs in the same year. The Company continued to expand its facilities and operations to include a storehouse, engine foundry, brass foundry and sawmill; the Company acted as a forwarder and broker. By 1838, the N H and

D Company employed 400 men making it perhaps the largest shipbuilding facility in Upper Canada. In 1840, it purchased land in Chippawa and opened a branch operation there.

The Company encountered hard times as the supply of steamers outpaced demand. In 1841, one of the Company's backers, the Suspension Bridge Bank, failed. The Company extended credit to Donald Bethune for five vessels it constructed, but he went bankrupt in 1848, leaving the NH and D Company £25,000 in debt and it went into trusteeship in that year. Clark Gamble was the new trustee and under him shipbuilding resumed. In 1853, Samuel Zimmerman, a prominent railway promoter in the province bought the company. He extended the railway from Queenston to Niagara, put up a station on the wharf, and began a railroad car factory. By 1861, the Company had built thirty-five steamboats, twelve schooners, three propeller-driven boats, one gunboat and more than eighteen barges. Within a few years, steamboat travel began to decline as the railway network expanded and the Company built fewer and fewer ships until it collapsed in 1864 with the property being subdivided and sold off in 1870.

In 1877, the Niagara Navigation Company was formed. It purchased the vessels *Chicora*, *Cibola*, *Chippewa*, *Corona*, and *Cayuga* for the Niagara-Toronto run. The *Cibola*, *Chippewa*, and *Cayuga* were considered "floating palaces," a fitting link to the elegance of the Queen's Royal Hotel and other town properties. More than 10,000 visitors arrived on some weekends. The *Cayuga* was built in 1906 and by its last run in 1957, Fifteen million visitors had sailed on it. Canada Steamship Lines bought the company in 1916. The steamboat era ended in 1957 when the *Cayuga* made its final run.

There were many ancillary businesses located near the dockyard - a tanners, brewery and a sail making enterprise. Other industries developed included an axe factory, lumber and planing mills, "a pop factory," a soap and candle factory, a barrel factory, "an apple evaporator," a slaughter house, a lime kiln, a brickyard and "a willow basket business." (Masters in "Niagara Reminiscences"). Like many other Ontario towns with good transportation links, NOTL was a very busy industrial centre.

The railway (Erie and Ontario) reached NOTL in 1854 and enabled a growing number of farmers to send their products to market either by rail or by ship from the town. Some farms even had their own sidings. Since this was the town's only railway connection to the rest of the country, it was strongly supported locally, e.g., the township purchased its shares and even lent money to the company. From the 1880s to the 1920s, "Six passenger trains a day used this line to carry passengers and freight to the docks at Niagara." (Jackson & Burtniak, 173) By 1907, the Michigan Central Railway owned the line. In 1914, the Electric Railway started and continued until 1931. The local station remains on King Street.

In the 1920s and 1930s, the popularity of the automobile further reduced the passenger steamship business. In 1939, Shepherd Boat Works operated at the former NH & D Company site. This company was bought out by Mr. James Hahn in 1958, and later by Trojan Yachts of Lancaster, Pennsylvania who eventually closed the plant in 1978. Other boatbuilders who have come – and some have gone - include Grew, C & C Yachts, Hinterhoeller, Neptunus and Turner.

The basin was converted to a marina and since 1979 it has been operated by the NOTL Sailing Club. Nearby, Scotty Murray Boat Repair started in 1966 and continues still.

The founders of the NH & D Company have left us a wonderful legacy: a basin that is still intact, the 1834 storehouse now used by the NOTL Sailing Club for offices and clubhouse, the recently restored Niagara Harbour and Dock Company Office (154 Ricardo St.) of c.1835 and the Woodruff House on Ball street which shares with the office the interesting detail of a "top hat door" with an extraordinarily high doorway so that customers could enter without removing their "stovepipe" hats.

References:

"Niagara Reminiscences" by Joseph E. Masters on http://historyniagara.niagara.com

B. Parker, "The Niagara Harbour and Dock Company," Ontario History, 72 (June, 1980), 93-118

4.4 Tourism

NOTL's history, architecture, scenery and cultural attractions have been major reasons for tourists to visit the town and area. Prominent early visitors included Patrick Campbell 1792, the Duc de La Rochefoucauld-Liancourt in 1795, Isaac Weld in 1796 and George Heriot in 1800. As a cultural activity, tourism has been important to this town from very early times so that in this respect, this is another leadership role in Ontario. Tourism in NOTL was also related to interest in Niagara Falls, "where the tourist industry began, not only in Ontario but in North America." (Jasen, 29) By the 1790s visitors were coming in increasing numbers and they usually passed by or through NOTL either on their way to the Falls or on their departure down Lake Ontario and the St. Lawrence. After the War of 1812, visitors also came to see battlefield sites including Fort George. As transportation improved with steamboats and trains, people came to the town particularly in the summer to escape the pressures of business, to improve their health or simply to enjoy the pleasures of a small town with its access to the lake and river. People still come here for those reasons as well as for the many historical features that remain. Again, this pattern in tourism indicates what has happened elsewhere in Canada.

Inns (or taverns or hotels or public houses) soon appeared in the town to accommodate and serve both residents and visitors. By 1794, there were "at least six taverns" (Capital Years, 200) and their proliferation may have been a strong incentive for the legislature to pass an act to license "Public Houses," and the selling of liquor. By the 1830s, travelers could eat and sleep at the Angel Inn (c.1825), the Whale Inn (1835) and the Moffat Hotel (1835), which all exist today.

In 1869, the majestic Queen's Royal Hotel opened its doors to a wealthy clientele, including international visitors. It fronted Lake Ontario and offered beautiful vistas amidst tennis courts and lawn bowling greens. World Tennis Tournaments were played here. The world-class hotel tradition in NOTL stems from this property which, sadly, closed down in 1925 as a result of financial difficulties. It was dismantled and in its place we have the green slopes and trees of the Queen's Royal Park which is a popular spot for picnics, walking dogs and observing life.

Other hotel properties cropped up to accommodate the increasing flow of visitors: Prince of Wales (c.1882), Chautauqua Hotel (1891) and Oban House (1895). The golden era of trains subsided with the popularity of the automobile and finally died with the coming of the Great Depression. The old town's revival waited until the 1970s, largely the result of an interest in heritage preservation and of the creation of the Shaw Festival (1962). This was the brainchild of a local lawyer, Brian Doherty.

The Shaw Festival, now in its 38th year, attracted 320,000 patrons in 1999 and involves three theatres including the Court House (1847). The Festival is world-renowned and boasts the second largest repertory theatre in North America. It attracts a large portion of our stay-over business today and is a key contributor to the success of many of our business sectors.

The commercial Heritage District is focused on Queen Street, with approximately 105 restaurants and shops in a four-block area. Many of the buildings are 19th century. Our Local Architectural Conservation Advisory Committee (LACAC) has a strong influence in heritage preservation in this district.

References

Agriculture and Farm Life in the Niagara Peninsula. Proceedings of the Fifth Annual Niagara Peninsula History Conference (1983)
Bicentennial Stories of Niagara-on-the-Lake. Edited by John L. Field (Lincoln, Ont: 1981)
J. Carnochan, History of Niagara (Facsimile edition, 1973)
The Capital Years. Niagara-on-the-Lake, 1792-1796. Edited by Richard Merritt, Nancy Butler, and Michael Power. (Toronto; Dundurn Press, 1991)
Dictionary of Canadian Biography, 8 (James Crooks), 9 (Donald Bethune)
J.N.Jackson and J.Burtniak, Railways in the Niagara Peninsula (Belleville: Mika, 1978)
P. Jasen, Wild Things. Nature, Culture, and Tourism in Ontario, 1790-1914 (U of T Press, 1995), especially chap. 2
Isabelle Ridgway, Sailing out of Niagara...since 1833

GARA RIVER LINE
THE SHORT PICTURESQUE TRIP TO TORONTO
4 TRIPS DAILY 4
Chicora

FORT GEORGE
National Historic Site
Walking Tour
MICHIGAN CENTR
BUFFALO & NIAGARA FALLS
ELECTRIC RAILWAY

POLITICAL, CULTURAL AND SOCIAL IMPORTANCE OF NIAGARA-ON-THE-LAKE

5.1 Political

In 1791 a new form of government was created by the British parliament for the colony of Canada. Under the Constitutional (or Canada) Act of that year, Canada (or Quebec) was to be divided into two and each section was to have its own legislature with both elected and appointed bodies. The result was a political watershed for both Lower Canada (now Quebec) and Upper Canada (now Ontario). It would be Ontario rather than Quebec that would provide the model in many political, social, cultural, economic and military aspects for Canadian settlements west of the Great Lakes. Within Ontario, Niagara-on-the-Lake (NOTL) would both lead in and reflect many aspects of the province's history, society, culture, and economy.

The political history of Ontario began in NOTL when the first lieutenant governor of Upper Canada inaugurated parliamentary government in the new colony. The initial session of the provincial parliament lasted from 17 September to 15 October, 1792, and saw the passage of the first legislation for Upper Canada. The new colony was significant for many reasons: Upper Canada was the first British inland colony, and, therefore, a model for all that followed in what is now Canada. Establishment of Upper Canada as an English-speaking colony meant an anglophone and a francophone government (the elected legislature in Lower Canada was dominated by French-speaking members) had to learn to work together in some areas, particularly, the distribution of customs duties. This was the first example of such cooperation in the British Empire and in North America. Therefore, as methods were worked out with significant stages in 1841, 1848 and 1867, they provided a model for future Canada. Central to this development was Upper Canada.

The first five sessions of Upper Canada's parliament met in NOTL and some of the legislation it passed was of basic significance: English common law, courts, and trial by jury were all established; another act provided for weights and measures. In 1793 the anti-slavery act was the first limitation on slavery in the British Empire which certainly contributed to the demise of slavery in Upper Canada. The passage of this act has been recognized by the HSMB. An act to provide for the appointment of parish and township officers meant the beginning of municipal government and an act for the maintenance of roads started our network of land transportation routes. 1794 saw passage of the first militia law, an act to regulate the practice of law and an act to establish a superior court. These laws meant the beginning of a resident civilian obligation to defend Upper Canada and the official recognition of the legal profession in the province. In 1795 an act approved the agreement with Lower Canada to divide the revenue derived from duties on imported wines and liquors; an act provided for the registration of deeds, conveyances and wills (this was to confirm land titles); an act was passed to regulate the practice of medicine ("physic and surgery"). In 1796 an act to regulate coinage was passed. Later that year the government moved to York (Toronto).

As an inland British colony, strongly influenced by the United States (a very different model of constitutional, legal, political, social and economic development), Upper Canada was an entirely new phenomenon. Its failure or absorption by the US probably would have meant Canada as we know it could not exist, i.e., beyond the ocean coasts and Quebec (the lower St. Lawrence). Its success indicated that a different nation could arise in the same continent as the United States.

The political, cultural and social history of Upper Canada evolved because of settlement by Americans (including Loyalists), native peoples and Europeans from the 1770s. A basic requirement for the new settlements was clear land title and the process of transferring ownership of native land to Crown began along Niagara River in the 1760s. Here (and along Detroit River) saw the beginning of treaties between Indians and the Crown to acquire land for settlers, a policy formally established by the Royal Proclamation of 1763 and which extended westward as Canada expanded in the 19th and 20th centuries. In the years 1783-84 the purchase of land from the Mississauga and Chippewa nations was confirmed and surveys were begun. [OHM, Map 4.2]

Although it ceased to be Upper Canada's capital, the town remained the District capital, which included administration for the counties of

Lincoln, Welland and Haldimand, and held the District Courthouse. In 1860, the county seat and courts were moved to St. Catharines, leaving NOTL without political significance. Its roles as provincial and then as county capital were ended, but the town had helped to launch Ontario's political development.

NOTL has witnessed events and people involved with political developments across the spectrum from a government side to opposition. Robert Gourlay became one of the first critics of the provincial government and was seen by later reformers as a martyr to the cause of political reform. When he arrived in Upper Canada in 1817, he stayed in the town with Thomas Clark, his wife's cousin, and in this district he found a good deal of discontent with the government. In January 1819, he was committed to the Niagara jail to await trial for disobeying an order under the Sedition Act. There he remained until 20 August when, having been found guilty, he was banished from Upper Canada. The treatment he suffered created the image of a much-wronged reformer and of a ruthless ruling group that could not accept any criticism. A leading figure in the postwar discontent was Robert Nichol who was not a resident of NOTL. Before the war, he was a prominent merchant who became well acquainted with Isaac Brock. When war broke out, Major-General Brock appointed Nichol quartermaster general of the militia and he took part in actions in and around NOTL. He was elected to the assembly for Norfolk, and by 1814 he was the government leader as well as holding local offices in Niagara. In the seventh parliament (1817-20), he became the government's leading critic, but because of his previous service on behalf of the government and his war record, he could not be dismissed as a mere malcontent. He gave opposition to the government a strong degree of respectability. These early critics contributed to the development of democratic government in Ontario, a long and varied process. One of the best-known figures in this story was William Lyon Mackenzie. He did not live in NOTL, but he resided close by in Queenston where he began his journalistic career, which led directly to his involvement in politics. In 1849 he visited the town after his return from exile.

5.2 Social

British-American society in Ontario can be dated from 1778 when John Butler was sent to begin farming on the west side of Niagara River to provide provisions for Fort Niagara's garrison and refugees there. The log buildings that his Rangers constructed marked the beginning of civilian occupation of the west bank of the Niagara. By the time the military's need for this enterprise ended, a permanent European-type settlement had been established, one that would have wide-ranging consequences for Canada. The activities of Butler's Rangers marked Niagara as "the first permanent British settlement in western Quebec." [HAC, II, Plate 7]

This was a multicultural society from the outset because American settlers had German, Dutch, French, Hungarian, African, English, Irish and Scottish ancestry. They were soon followed by immigrants from Europe. Meanwhile, native peoples continued to live in and near the town. Town residents ranged from poor to very rich and worked in many different trades and professions. In 19th century terms, all classes and races of people could be found here, often living side by side. Shortly after the War of 1812 ended, there was mass immigration from the British Isles to Upper Canada. So many Irish immigrants arrived that a section at the southeastern end of NOTL became known as Irishtown. Niagara was a terminus of the Underground Railroad resulting in a substantial black community in town with its own church. The variety of ethnic origins, languages and of occupations continues to the present day. Many other parts of Ontario, and of Canada, mirrored NOTL's experience some at about the same period, some later in time. In other words, socially the town became Canadian.

The first Freemasons' lodge in the province opened here in 1792. This fraternal order would expand throughout Upper Canada and, at times, in Ontario's history exert considerable influence.

Whether considered as a social or cultural aspect, there have always been religious variety and a good deal of cooperation among different churches in NOTL. In the 1790s there were Anglicans (Church of England) and Presbyterians and soon afterwards, congregations of Baptists, Roman Catholics, and Methodists appeared.

Assemblies (formal dances) were held every two weeks throughout the winter; the tradition of a New Year's Day levee was begun here by Simcoe.

One of the most distressful events for the town's population was the deliberate burning of the town on 10 December 1813. American troops had occupied the community since 27 May and by December, their commander decided the position was no longer tenable. Before he withdrew across the river, he gave the inhabitants very short notice to leave their homes before his men set them ablaze. His troops were aided by the Canadian Volunteers, a corps led by and recruited from Canadian residents. In effect, the men of this unit were destroying the homes and businesses of former neighbors. The town ceased to exist and it says much for the robustness of its society that as early as 1815 people began to rebuild their homes and their social life quickly regained its vigor.

5.3 Cultural

The town plot was laid out in 1791 according to 18th century concepts of town-planning and NOTL retains that pattern so that its roads and buildings show continuity of settlement from the early 19th century to the present. Its structures and streetscapes display the intermingling of residential housing -both wealthy and modest- as well as business, governmental, and military buildings. But the town is not a museum. It is a living community that continues to change to suit the needs of its residents.

The first newspaper in Ontario was published here on 13 April 1793 under the title "The Upper Canada Gazette or American Oracle." [HAC, II, Plate 51] Newspapers played many important roles in pioneer society (equivalent today to TV, radio and newspapers) not only for news and opinions of all sorts, but also for advertising and for the development of literacy. The beginning of this development in NOTL shows the town's importance at that time. Upper Canada's first Agricultural Society was formed here in 1792. Beginning in 1793, the first country fall fair, a very important institution in an agricultural community, became an annual event here on the second Monday of October.

In 1797, the Law Society of Upper Canada was founded in NOTL in order to regulate lawyers and provide practical experience for law clerks. By providing for a self-regulating legal profession, this Society represents an important step in the province's legal history. Taken in conjunction with the early establishment of a newspaper, an agricultural society and a library, these developments indicate cultural leadership of the new province by NOTL.

On 8 June 1800, forty-one Niagara citizens formed a subscription library. The Record Book of the library's initial book collection and its borrowers still exists in the Niagara Historical Society's Museum. Most of the books were destroyed during the War of 1812, but the library was revived after the war and has continued to flourish ever since. It is one of the cultural centres of the community.

Niagara has been home to writers, artists and other creative people such as, William Kirby, Janet Carnochan, Brian Doherty, Jacobine Jones, Veronica Tennant, Trisha Romance, Christopher Newton, Tony Van Bridge, Campbell Scott and many others. Kirby was editor of a local newspaper, the Niagara Mail, from 1871 to 1895 and a charter member of the Royal Society of Canada. He was also the author of several poems and of other writings, but it was for his novel, The Golden Dog (1877; translated into French 1884) that he gained a reputation outside of Canada. A modern example of cultural leadership is the Shaw Festival that has grown from small beginnings to become one of Canada's major professional theatre festivals.

Townsfolk have been in the forefront of heritage preservation and the results can be seen in the town's heritage of buildings, streetscapes and organizations. Also, Memorial Hall of the Niagara Historic Society's Museum, dating from 1907, is the oldest building in Ontario erected specifically as a museum. In sports, NOTL has the oldest golf course in Ontario (from 1878). The first International Golf tournament for men and women was held here in 1895.

Religious events centered in NOTL have had wide implications. A conference, later known as "The Niagara Bible Conference" held its meetings from 1883 to 1897. "It was here the modern prophetic conference as we know it today in North America had its beginning." (Unger in Bicentennial Stories, 76) Participants came from Canada,

Great Britain and the United States and represented many Christian denominations: Anglicans, Baptists, Episcopalians, Methodists, Presbyterians, and Plymouth Brethren.

At the western edge of the old town is an area known as Niagara Chautauqua. It was built in the 1880s upon the model of the American Chautauqua at Jamestown, New York. The streets were laid out like the spokes of a wheel, radiating from a central circle where a large amphitheatre was built capable (it was claimed) of seating 4,000 people. The aim of the Niagara Chautauqua was to hold summer meetings "for Literary, Social, and Scientific purposes." (Niagara Advance, Spring 1971, p.8). People stayed in tents or cottages and attended courses, lectures, conferences and Sunday services, and also enjoyed various forms of recreation, e.g., baseball, tennis, croquet and lawn bowling, and a sandy beach. A wharf was built out into the lake for steamers to bring in people and a special railway spur line was laid across town to provide railway connections to Buffalo, NY, and beyond. The Chautauqua declined because of financial difficulties and suffered a major blow when the large Chautauqua Hotel burned down in August 1909. The street layout remains, along with some of the original houses, and street names like Addison, Shakespeare, Luther, Wesley and Wilberforce may still inspire. The Niagara Chautauqua was probably the largest one in Canada. It was certainly a unique cultural and social feature of NOTL and its legacy can still be seen.

References

The Capital Years. Ed. by R. Merritt, N. Butler, and M. Power (1991)
Bicentennial Stories. Edited by John L. Field (1981)
Dictionaries of Canadian Biography, vols. 6 (Robert Nichol) and 9 (Robert Gourlay, W.L. Mackenzie)
HAC Historical Atlas of Canada
Niagara Advance, Historical Issue, Spring 1971
OHM Ontario's History in Maps

BUILT HERITAGE

6.1 The Layout

Newark (now Niagara-on-the-Lake) was one of several late 18th century planned government towns which straddled the southern fringe of Upper Canada, along its frontier with the United States. Characteristically it was laid out with the military precision of a gridiron.

It differs from most of the others in its generous layout of four-acre blocks separated by chain (66'-O") wide streets, with some wider cross streets of a chain and a half. Chosen as the first capital of the new province of Upper Canada this generous layout catered to the demands of its military, commercial and ceremonial functions. The town was almost completely surrounded by open space in the form of defensive military reserves and most of these reserves have been preserved by Parks Canada.

The original town plot set up in 1791 was divided into one-acre lots and in 1794 the lots between Queen Street and the waterfront were subdivided into half-acre lots. Reserves were made for churches and schools and a central square set apart within the wider streets of Mary and William, and Mississauga and Butler. Ultimately, however, the people did not adapt to the new plan and Queen became the main commercial street.

The original town plot was extended subsequently by the addition of the 'New Survey' to the east of King Street in 1823, on part of the Military Reserve exchanged for an area elsewhere originally owned by the Hon. James Crooks. The layout of square blocks was similar, some having mid-block lanes, but the subdivision into building plots was somewhat miscellaneous. The old Town area also included an area described as "Irishtown" in the southeast quadrant, where the second Courthouse of 1817 was located. The original Black community tended to occupy the southern end of the old Town. Their presence today is marked by a few older houses and by a

National Historic Sites and Monuments plaque to the 1793 Anti-slavery legislation as well as a Provincial heritage marker that commemorates the Negro Burial Ground near Mary and Mississauga Streets.

6.2 Historic Periods

Illustrations survive and various travelers' accounts confirm the fine features of some of the early building of Newark including Deputy Surveyor-General D.W. Smith's House, later Government House, which occupied the Queen/King/Johnson/Regent block. This block was later the basis of town-owned land, largely privately developed, except for the Courthouse site including Market Square behind. Early buildings also included the first brick house in Ontario, built by the Honourable William Dickson, dated 1795 and a c.1811 Regency bungalow by the same owner, both destroyed in the razing of Newark in 1813 during the War of 1812.

The citizens of the town, despite government encouragement otherwise, wished to rebuild in the original location, many constructing houses on sites of destroyed buildings. Only the walls of St. Mark's Church (1804-1809) survived, but the building was reconstructed by 1822. It took the Presbyterians, who had built a timber church about 1794, until 1831 to replace theirs in brick.

As the town rebuilt in the immediate postwar years, the pattern saw variety and intermix of uses - taverns alongside houses and structures housing other ancillary occupations such as liveries and workshops. Not only did building uses differ, but also did size, shape and individual design, though early examples subscribed to the neo-Classical Vernacular in the last regard. This style was ordered, well-proportioned, dignified yet intimate. In the central part of the town there are still a number of these early streetscapes and several distinctive and distinguished groups of buildings, most notably the pairs of hip-roofed houses of the 1830s on Johnson Street flanking Regent and Victoria Streets, and on the latter corner a brick one of 1835.

The main street, Queen, commercial for only four blocks, also exhibits a great variety in the core area, both as to the uses and buildings. Later infilling and more recent conversions have tended to blend the effect, though the visual result is still notably varied.

As subdivision of earlier and larger holdings progressed, newer houses in later building styles contributed to the scene: Gothic Revival appears and the later Victorian eclectic designs including the so-called Queen Anne Revival and plainer Edwardian examples. Even a few modern or freshly contemporary structures by architects and designers have appeared like the new Post Office. A late Victorian and Edwardian complement of great summer houses, mostly along western Queen Street, as well as the dramatic enlargement and later adornment of early houses such as those along eastern John Street, contribute to the architectural and historical variety and interest.

The concentration of early buildings of note within such a relatively small area prompted the Federal Government's National Historic Sites Division to undertake a Pilot Study for the National Inventory of Historic Building in the early 1960s. As a result, an illustrated glossary of historical/architectural terms, The Architecture of the Town and Township of Niagara - Niagara Foundation 1967, was prepared. In 1971 Old Niagara on the Lake (University of Toronto Press) with drawings by Robert Montgomery made a choice from the selection done earlier in the Pilot Study. Although many of these buildings survive, some have been lost and several others sadly altered to lose their valuable and original detail, thus compromising their integrity and damaging their intrinsic value.

6.3 Streetscapes

The earlier tendency to build close to the street persisted so that the street width was expressed physically. Later subdivision and a growing preference for front yards produced an extraordinary effect of enclosure and receding streetscape still to be appreciated today. This was enhanced by the notable predilection for fences and hedges enclosing front gardens, a characteristic now tending to break down as fences became due for renewal and an admiration of a weed-free sward sweeping up to the entrance front follows the more modern taste. But it is the alternately expanding and contracting street spaces which give the old Town its special quality. Add to this a magnificent tree-scape, much of it formed by plantings of silver maple of more than a century ago by Henry Paffard, pharmacist and mayor. These magnificent trees embrace the streets with their canopies and the older soft edges of graveled shoulders and greened boulevards combine to give a tranquil effect. This aspect of the old Town is a remarkable survival.

The commercial core still illustrates earlier developments of main streets with buildings erected to suit individual merchant's needs rather than those erected as commercial blocks by entrepreneurs to offer as rental space. Niagara-on-the-Lake offers a variety of architectural styles while other main streets feature the uniformity of the commercial block facades. Here, separations between buildings and frequent lane access to rear yards are common. So too the size and height of buildings differ widely. Some, such as the Liquor Store, were enlarged in the mid-nineteenth century to be more appropriate to the new Courthouse of 1846 alongside. Most are two storeys; some even three. A few single storey buildings tend to be later extensions to earlier buildings or more modern replacements.

6.4 Conclusion

Niagara's real story is one of boom, providing the means and incentive to create the wonders it still expresses, followed by bust which tended to conserve it. Here are some stages:

- First capital, military post, transhipment point
- Loss of capital status (moderated by its continuation as regional centre and county seat)
- Razing of Town 1813; Post-War of 1812 rebuilding
- Industrial development (Niagara Harbour and Dock Company 1831) creation of harbour, other industries, lake traffic, steam railway extension to Erie and Ontario c.1854
- Loss of county seat to St. Catharines in 1862
- Collapse of Niagara Harbour and Dock Company, 1862

- Resort eras from late 1860s on; building of Queen's Royal Hotel, lake transportation /railway connection; development of Chautauqua
- World War I: Niagara as a military camp area
- Post World War I and decline of Niagara as special resort, demolition of Queen's Royal Hotel, the Great Depression, lake and rail transportation succumb to automobiles
- World War II: again a training ground, but only a modest infusion
- Post World War II: doldrums, loss of railway, steamer traffic
- From early 1970s Niagara becomes a tourist destination

Old Fort, Niagara-on-the-Lake, Canada

Coca-Cola
DRUGS
DRUGS

Miss J. Carnochan
H.M. Public School 1872–

Much that has determined the history and preserved the heritage of Niagara-on-the-Lake is due to the actions of its citizens. This strong, continuous involvement with their community is evident in: the siting of the colonial settlement, its development, and its boundaries; the citizens' defence of the Common along with other historic sites and cultural landscapes; the safeguarding and restoration of heritage buildings; and, the preservation of streetscapes and viewplanes.

7.1 The Siting and Nature of the Colonial Settlement and the Determination of Its Boundaries

In the Fall of 1779, Sir Frederick Haldimand, Governor of Quebec, asked Lt.Col. Bolton to arrange for people to cultivate "land about the Fort [Fort Niagara]...[to supply] the post with bread." Colonel John Butler organized non-combatant refugees to cross to the west bank of the Niagara River to plant crops in what had been determined to be fertile soil on a plain which may have been the site of Neutral cornfields. The expectation was that these men could return to their old homes once the rebellion (American Revolution) was put down. No titles were given to the land despite efforts by the settlers to encourage the authorities to approve some type of tenure for the west bank farmers. Without waiting for government approval, Colonel Butler commissioned Allan Macdonell (McDonell) to carry out a survey with names, an act for which he was criticized for having exceeded his authority.

In 1783 the Rebellion ended with the Thirteen Colonies gaining independence and the new settlers of Niagara unwilling to return to the new republic. When, in March of 1784, Lieutenant William Tinling's survey indicated "the high ground from Navy Hall to the 4 Mile" was reserved for the Crown, Tinling had problems with Colonel Butler and four or five officers who had already settled there along with eighty or so other disbanded men who had "grabbed" water frontage and refused to surrender it. The new surveyor, Philip Frey, encountered similar problems; he complained in 1787 that "settlers changed property with impunity." He left the area having failed to correct "irregularities allowed early settlers upon government lands."

Colonel Butler relayed the complaints of farmers concerning insecure tenure to Major Matthews, and in 1788, the Land Board was created. In 1790, that board finally confirmed the original lines on the river front as per Macdonell's survey in order not to "derange the whole settlement," and in April of that year, the government issued plans for the town and the township.

The settlers demanded a voice in the proposed plans, and despite the efforts of the Land Board, the settlers could not be persuaded to vacate their land which had been selected for the town site. Four options were proposed and voted upon at a meeting of the militia. As a result, the Crown Lands south of Navy Hall were selected for the town, but since there was not enough river frontage, the site was moved to the northwest of Navy Hall.

In 1791, Augustus Jones undertook a land survey, but Colonel Butler and other settlers refused "expropriation," with the result that a triangle of approximately 40 acres was excluded from D.W. Smith's 1784 plan.

After the razing of the town in 1813, the residents rebuilt where they wished to, ignoring government plans to the contrary. The citizens of the settlement were responsible for determining much, if not most, of the physical character of the Town. They demonstrated the spirit of independent thought and action which characterized the citizens from those early days to the present.

7.2 The Public's Defence of the Common, Other Historic Sites and Cultural Landscapes

In May of 1797, citizens of the town, suspecting that the Honourable William Dickson had designs on the Fort George Military Reserve, mounted a spirited public defense to protect what they regarded as "common" land, and which came to be known as "The Common."

In the late 1890s townsfolk petitioned the Canadian Government to preserve Navy Hall and in 1920, the Niagara Historical Society, led by its president, Janet Carnochan, "pressured the Niagara Parks Commission into improving Butler's Burial Ground, both the state of the site and the road that led to it." (Field, Carnochan, 50) The Historical Society went on to erect historic markers to historic sites and events in Niagara.

In the 1970s, the site of a home for the new Shaw Festival Theatre became very controversial. Proposals to site the theatre on the Fort Mississauga grounds, Queens Royal Park and the area behind the historic Courthouse were brought forward by the Shaw Board only to be turned down by Parks Canada or by Town Council. A compromise was developed whereby the new facility would be located on a corner of the Commons. While supported by many, this solution along with a decision to locate a nursing home on a portion of this historic property was opposed by those who felt that nothing should be done that would reduce the size of the open Commons.

In the past, anything which has been proposed which could potentially change the nature of the Old Town has met with close scrutiny by local heritage activists. Everything from the installation of curbs and gutters on heritage streets to the installation of parking meters on Queen Street has resulted in controversy, opposed by those who question any development which is perceived to detract from the historic appearance of the town. There is a fine balance between heritage preservation and the changes which are inevitable in a dynamic community and varying opinions of what does and does not constitute appropriate development. What makes Niagara-on-the-Lake unusual is that most residents and their elected representatives value the town's heritage but not all agree on the approaches that should be taken to ensure its preservation. Many residents have strong opinions and are more than willing to make their opinions known.

The town's rich past has led to the requirement that archaeological surveys be undertaken at any development planned for areas which are considered historically sensitive. Developers of several properties including the original homestead of the town's founder, John Butler, have been required to fund archaeological investigations of these properties. Recently, the Town commissioned an Archaeological Master Plan which maps out areas of potential archaeological sensitivity to ensure that all plans for development on potentially sensitive lands are surveyed by an archaeologist prior to construction. This is a major breakthrough in heritage preservation.

7.3 Heritage Preservation

Niagara-on-the-Lake has several groups and organizations which are centred on heritage preservation.

The Niagara Historical Museum and Society is a vibrant entity that mounts exhibits, conducts workshops, holds lectures, and keeps the public aware of Niagara-on-the-Lake's rich heritage. Dedicated volunteers have raised vast sums of money to preserve and enhance the Museum. The Museum consists of Memorial Hall, the first building constructed in Ontario as a museum and the old Grammar School. The society maintains an incredible collection related to Niagara's early history.

Another local organization, the Niagara Foundation, has been responsible for saving heritage properties. It began with the acquisition of the Niagara Apothecary which was restored through federal and provincial funding and refurnished by the Ontario College of Pharmacists. The Foundation continued with the conservation of the Fog-horn Keeper's House, the leasing and repairing of St. Mark's Rectory and, most recently, the purchase of the Stewart House, a small cottage built by one of Niagara's early Black citizens. This group of volunteers has worked relentlessly to raise money and undertake the stewardship of vulnerable historic buildings. Their annual house tours not only raise the necessary funds but have helped to make thousands of participants more aware of the town's rich heritage.

The Town's LACAC, a committee of volunteers appointed by Council to advise on heritage matters, comments upon all building applications in the town's designated Heritage District and offers advice, often coupled with on-site visits, to those who ask for it. What is important here is that very capable people, often with a good deal of expertise, have willingly volunteered to serve on the committee and have given a great deal of their time to its work of maintaining the town's historic integrity.

The Niagara Conservancy is one of the most vocal of the heritage-related groups, keeping a sharp eye on Town developments and challenging anything which it feels negatively impacts on the town's heritage character.

The Town's official historian, a volunteer, provides valuable assistance to citizens who wish to know the history of their property, possibly as a prelude to their asking for a historic designation; to archaeologists in finding out where to look for possible sites (such as the Butler Homestead); and to organizations and individuals looking for historical data.

The Friends of Fort George, a volunteer association that supports Parks Canada through its programs, activities, workshops and major events, helps to keep Niagara's heritage alive. This group was one of the first such co-operating associations in Canada. The Friends spearheaded a committee to organize a re-enactment of the landing of Lieutenant-Governor Simcoe at Navy Hall and the re-enactment of the first Parliament of Upper Canada. This was the premier venue for celebrating Ontario's Heritage Years, organized and funded by community volunteers, Parks Canada and the Town. Recently, the Friends of Fort George launched a millennium project to provide well marked and easier public access to Fort Mississauga National Historic Site and a public walking trail along the nearby lakeshore. Interpretive markers enhance the presentation of the stories of Fort Mississauga and the Point Mississauga Lighthouse, another National Historic Site. The project meets goals set a number of years ago by the Historic Sites and Monuments Board of Canada.

Credit must also be given to the private citizens who, over the years, have lovingly preserved and enhanced their historic houses and properties. In the 1990s, the town-owned pumphouse building was restored when a group of citizens approached the town to discuss the possible use of the building as an art centre. The Town organized meetings and staff from the Town Works and Recreation Departments worked with concerned volunteers, and the business community to raise the necessary funds. Today the Pumphouse is a thriving, exciting public place on the waterfront, hosting art exhibitions and teaching courses to children and adults.

One of the best examples of community action in preserving our heritage involved the Courthouse, a National Historic Site. All elements of the community and representatives from the Municipal, Provincial and Federal Governments, pulled together to raise the funds required to restore this vital part of the town's heritage. This was a major undertaking for a town the size of Niagara-on-the-Lake.

7.4 The Preservation of a Unique Culture

Niagara-on-the-Lake's history is inextricably bound up with the very active involvement of its citizens. For over two hundred-years the people have been in the forefront of the preservation of our precious heritage. These irreplaceable resources will continue to be guarded with much diligence.

This involvement and the actions taken by municipal, provincial and federal representatives in response to public concerns, have resulted in the preservation of much of the heritage that makes the Town unique.

REFERENCES

John L. Field, Janet Carnochan (Markham, Ont.: Fitzhenry & Whiteside, 1985)
Niagara Historical Society pamphlets

Niagara champion ..

Margherita Howe, O.C.

nd Mail

NFARE

GUIDE TO LIFE IN THE CITY PAGES 4 and 5

High cost

Opponents blame each oth

Board hears five appeals i

THE LADY of the lake

Of the millions who drank the water that flowed through The Niagara, only Margherita seemed to care

'We don't want changes

Howe, others tell committee development should be stopped

local news

Students don't want NOTL to become paradise lost

CAL

RO

Canadian

ographic

Senior profile

Margherita Howe

Niagara-on

Tensions rise over Queenston

Residents air concerns in face-to-face meeting with planners and aldermen

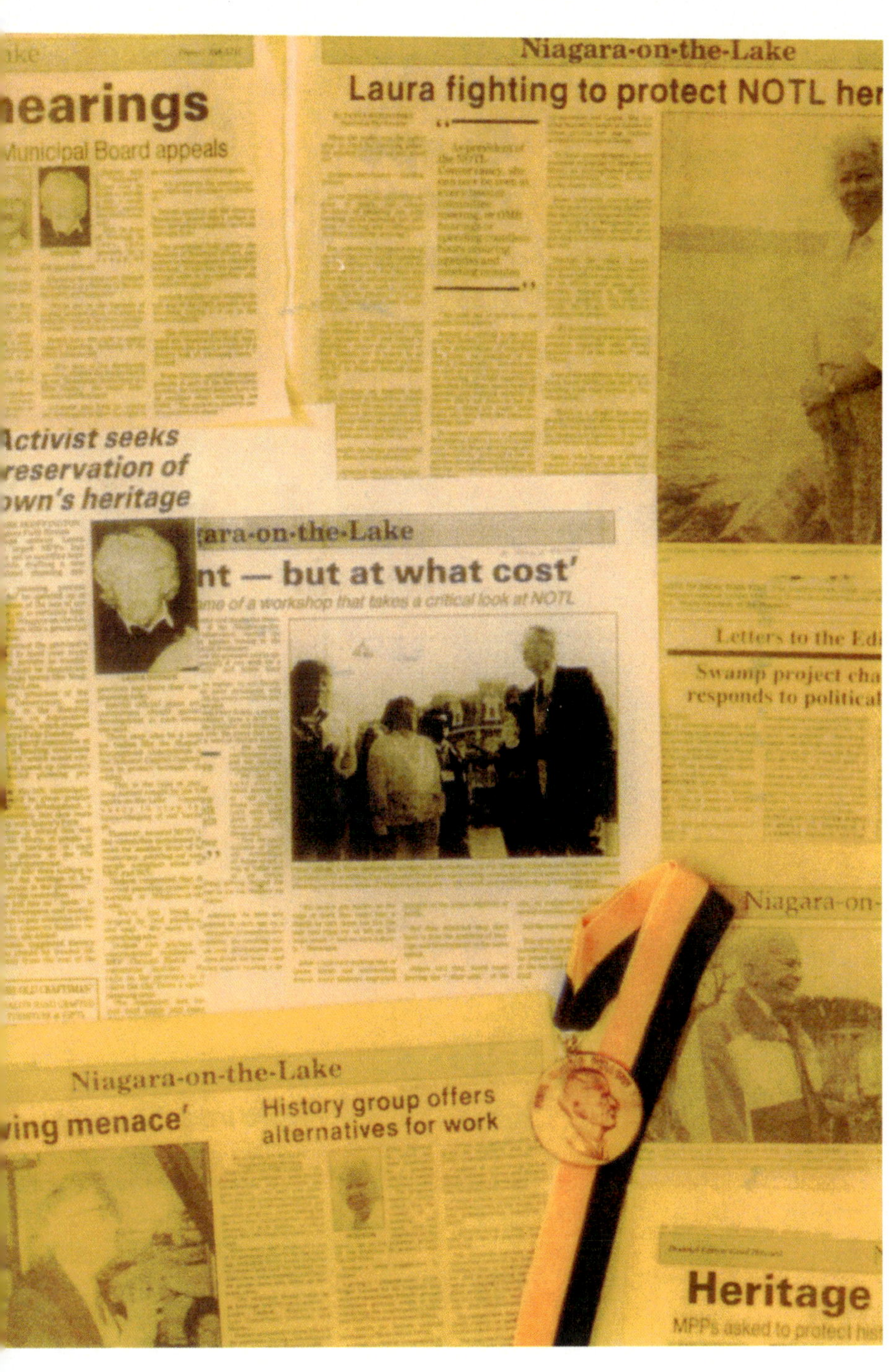

hearings
Municipal Board appeals
Niagara-on-the-Lake
Laura fighting to protect NOTL her
Activist seeks
reservation of
own's heritage
gara-on-the-Lake
nt — but at what cost'
me of a workshop that takes a critical look at NOTL
Letters to the Edi
Swamp project cha
responds to political
Niagara-on-
Niagara-on-the-Lake
ving menace'
History group offers
alternatives for work
Heritage
MPPs asked to protect his

HERITAGE DESIGNATION COMMITTEE
(1999 -   )

Richard Merritt
President, The Friends of Fort George National Historic Parks
Past President, Niagara Historical Society
Director, The Niagara Foundation

Erika Alexander
Executive Director, The Friends of Fort George
Past Chairman, Canadian Parks Partnership

Jim Alexander
Past Chairman, Niagara-on-the-Lake LACAC
Past Chairman, Community Heritage Ontario
Chairman, Niagara-on-the-Lake Citizens' Committee
for Ontario's Heritage Years (Simcoe's Landing 1992-1996)
Founding member and ad hoc Director of
The Friends of Fort George National Historic Parks Inc

Ron Dale
President, Niagara-on-the-Lake Chamber of Commerce
Board Member, Niagara Historic Society
Board Member, The Niagara Foundation

Laura Dodson
President, The Niagara-on-the-Lake Conservancy
Acting Chairman, Niagara-on-the-Lake Chapter of
The Ontario Archaeological Society
Acting Chairman, The Colonel John Butler Heritage Fund Committee

Norm Howe
Chairman, The Niagara Foundation

Steve Oprici
Vice-President, The Friends of Fort George National Historic Parks
Director, Niagara-on-the-Lake Association of Residents
Chairman, The Canada Day Celebrations
Past President, Niagara-on-the-Lake Chamber of Commerce
Past President, Queen Street Business Association
Former Director, Niagara Historical Society

Joy Ormsby
Official Historian, Town of Niagara-on-the-Lake
Member, Collection Management Committee
and Archival Committee of the Niagara Historical Society
Member, Niagara-on-the-Lake LACAC

Peter Stokes
Member, Niagara-on-the-Lake LACAC
Past President, Architectural Conservancy of Ontario
Author of books and studies on early Ontario architecture and towns

Les Taylor
Past President, Niagara Historical Society

Wesley Turner
Member, The Friends of Fort George National Historic Parks
Past President, St. Catharines Historical Society
Past President, Ontario Historical Society
Past Chairman, St. Catharines Historical Museum
Member, Board of the Canadian Canal Society

ACKNOWLEDGMENTS

The Shaw Festival Community Grant Programme

William Severin
Niagara Historical Society Museum

David Webb
Niagara National Historic Sites

Roy and Barbara Trantor

Don and Sally Read

First Great Seal of Upper Canada, March 28, 1792

The Friends of Fort George National Historic Park Inc.

P.O. Box 1283, Niagara-on-the-Lake, Ontario, L0S 1J0, Canada
ffg@computan.on.ca